The World of Supreme Persian Carpets

By Haji Mohamed Khan Zephyr Amil

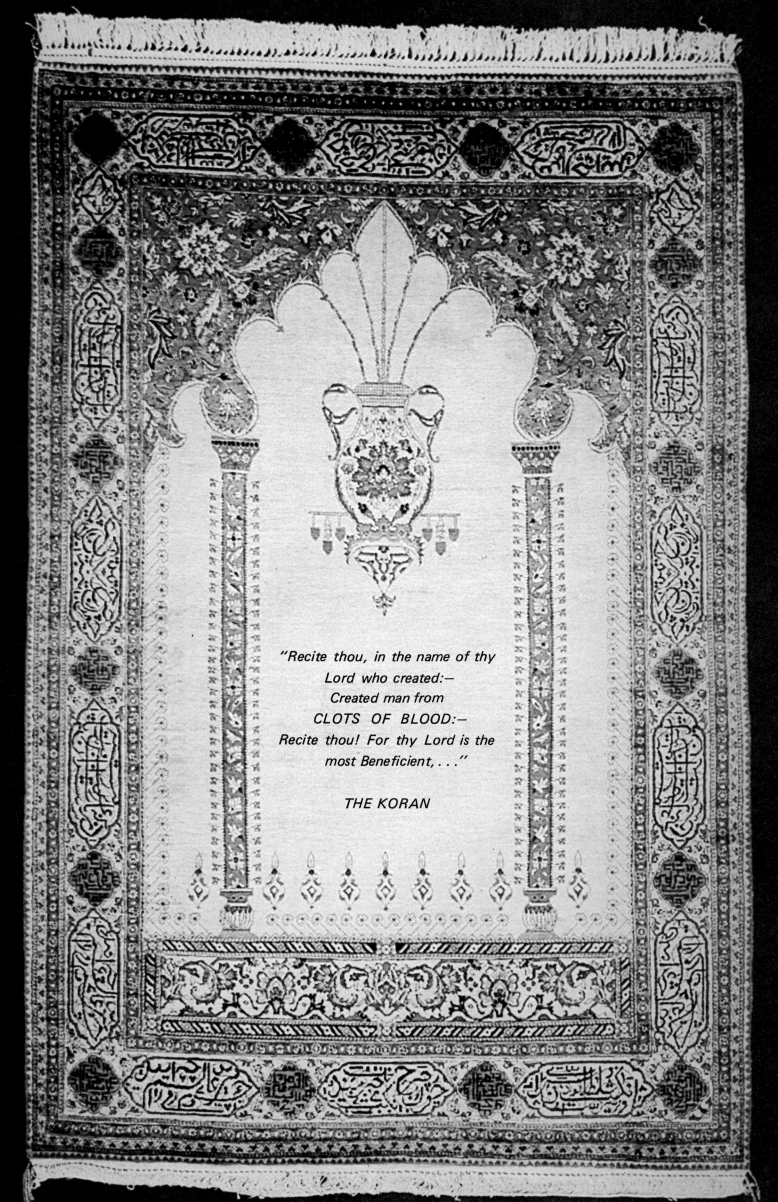

"Recite thou, in the name of thy
Lord who created:—
Created man from
CLOTS OF BLOOD:—
Recite thou! For thy Lord is the
most Beneficient, . . ."

THE KORAN

THIS BOOK IS
HUMBLY DEDICATED
TO THEIR IMPERIAL MAJESTIES
THE SHAHANSHAH
AND SHAHBANOU
AND THE PEOPLES
OF IRAN

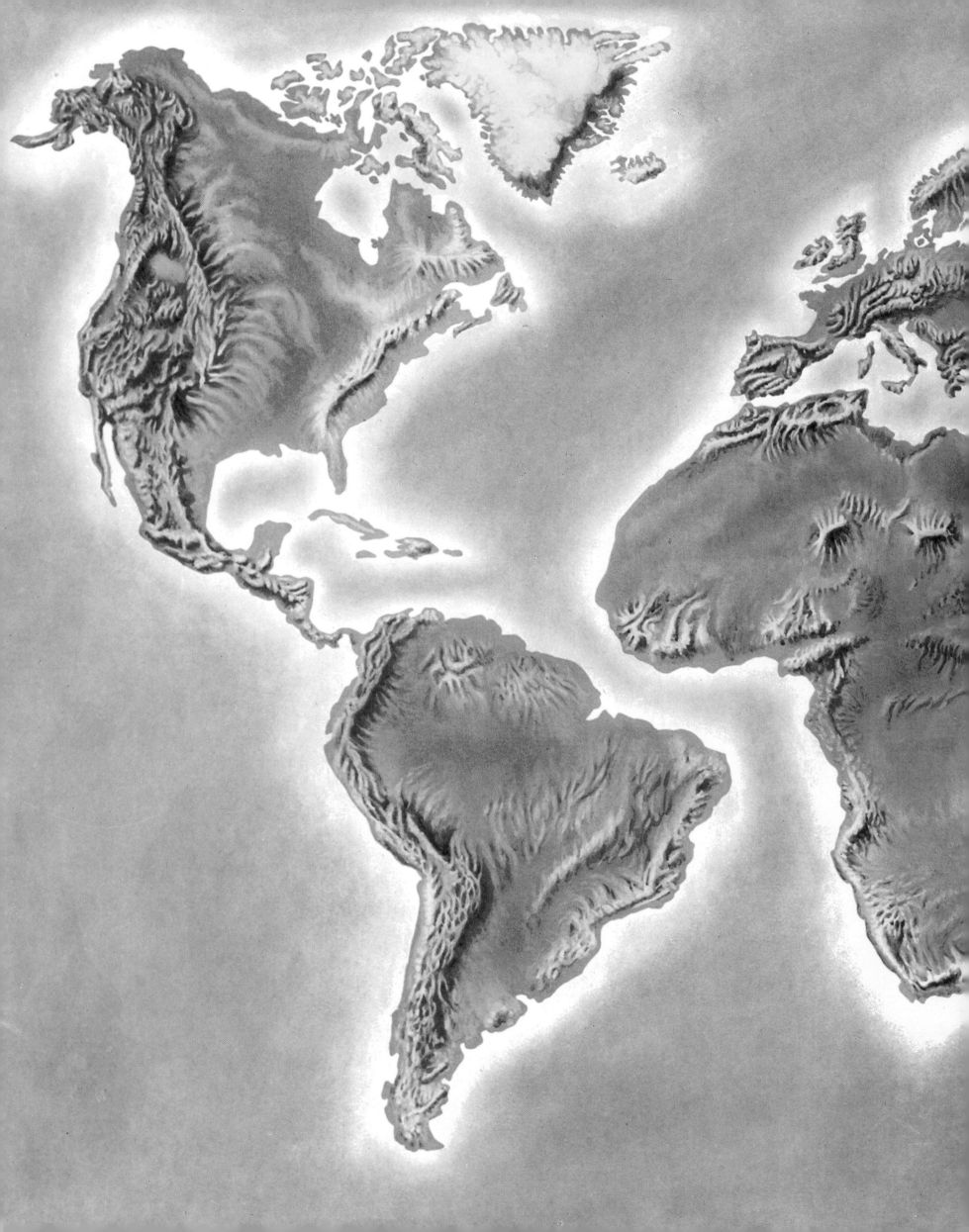

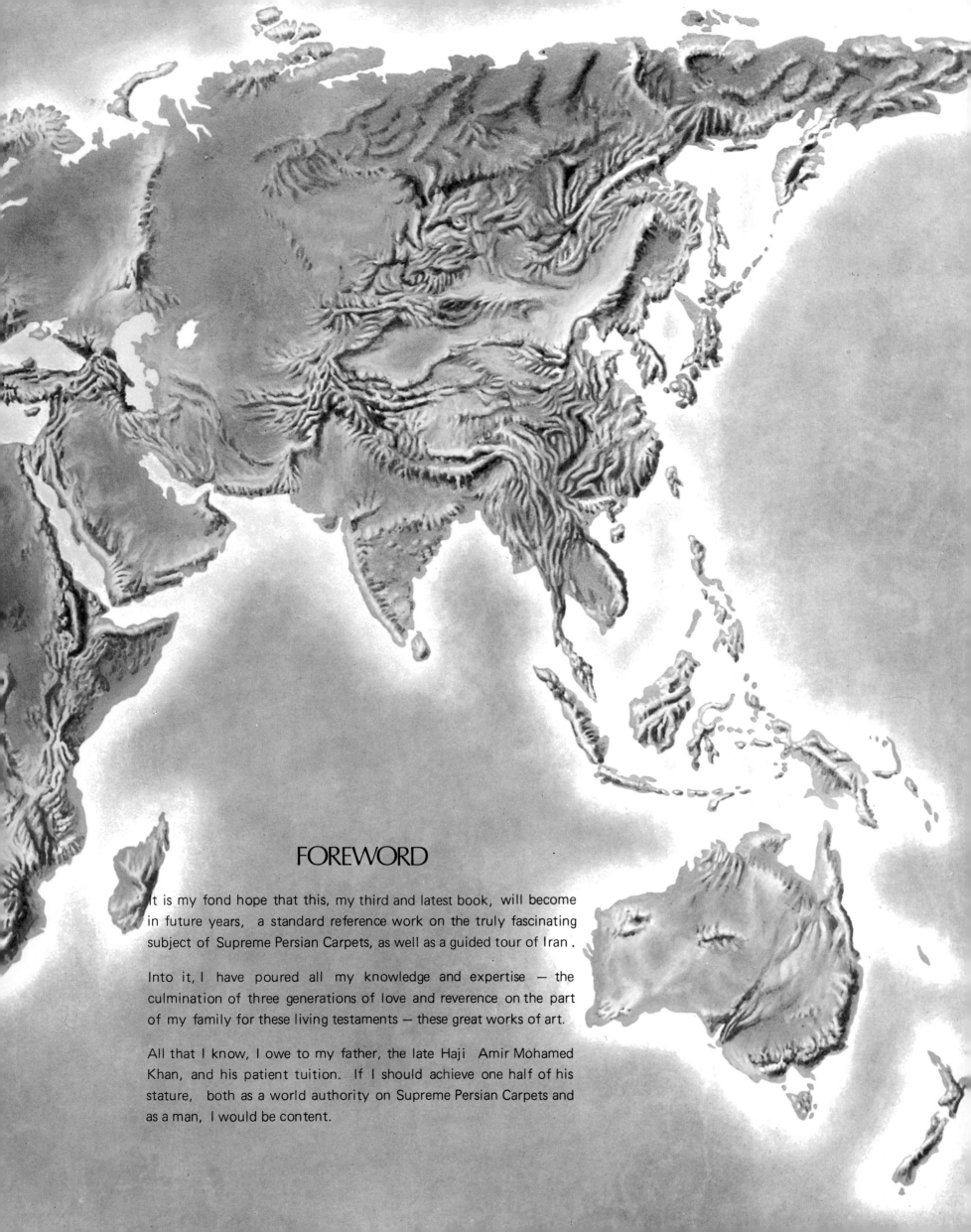

FOREWORD

It is my fond hope that this, my third and latest book, will become in future years, a standard reference work on the truly fascinating subject of Supreme Persian Carpets, as well as a guided tour of Iran.

Into it, I have poured all my knowledge and expertise — the culmination of three generations of love and reverence on the part of my family for these living testaments — these great works of art.

All that I know, I owe to my father, the late Haji Amir Mohamed Khan, and his patient tuition. If I should achieve one half of his stature, both as a world authority on Supreme Persian Carpets and as a man, I would be content.

*"Awake! for morning in the Bowl of Night
Has flung the Stone that puts the Stars to Flight:
And Lo! the Hunter of the East has caught
The Sultan's Turret in a Noose of Light"* . . .

Rubaiyat of OMAR KHAYYAM

CONTENTS

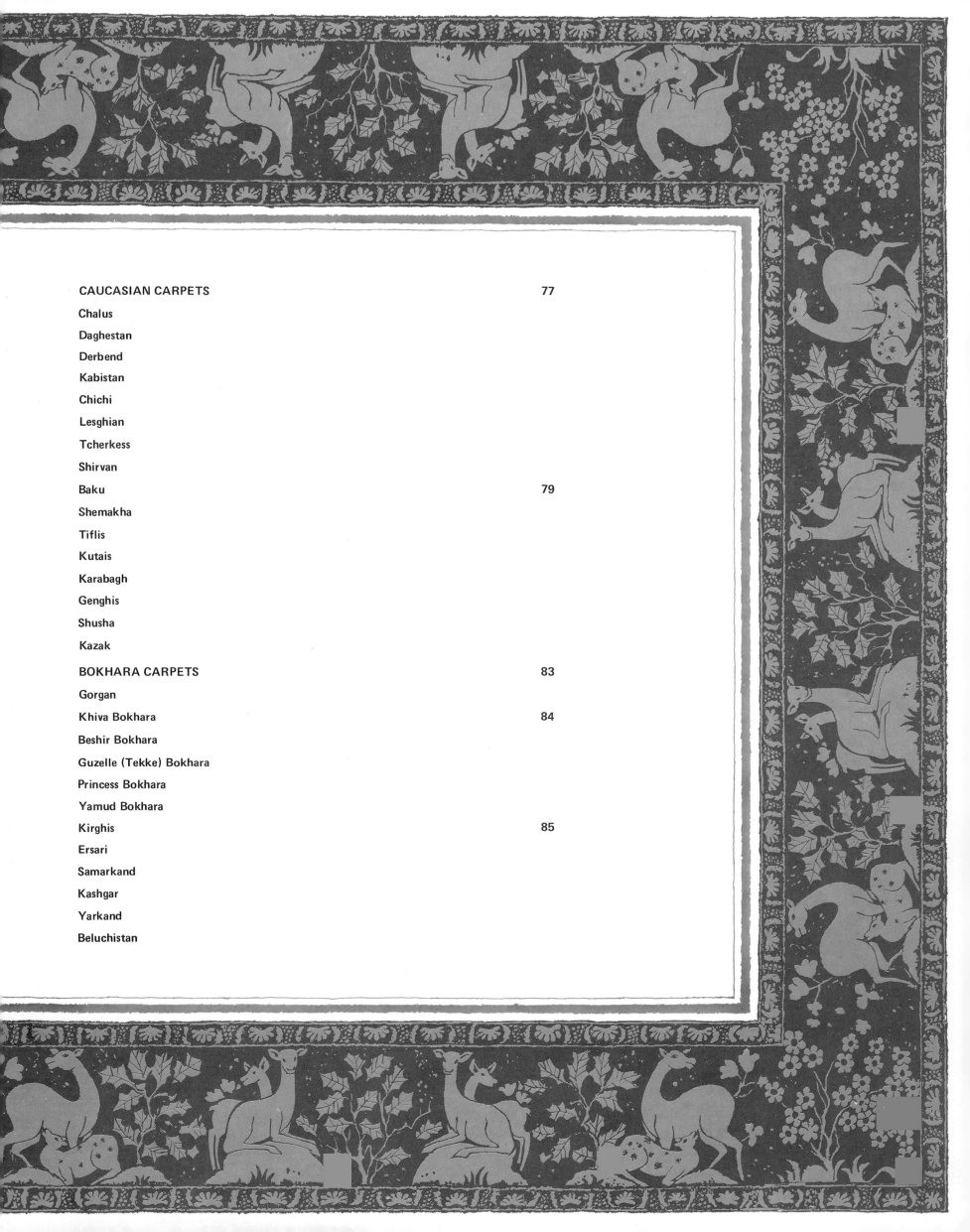

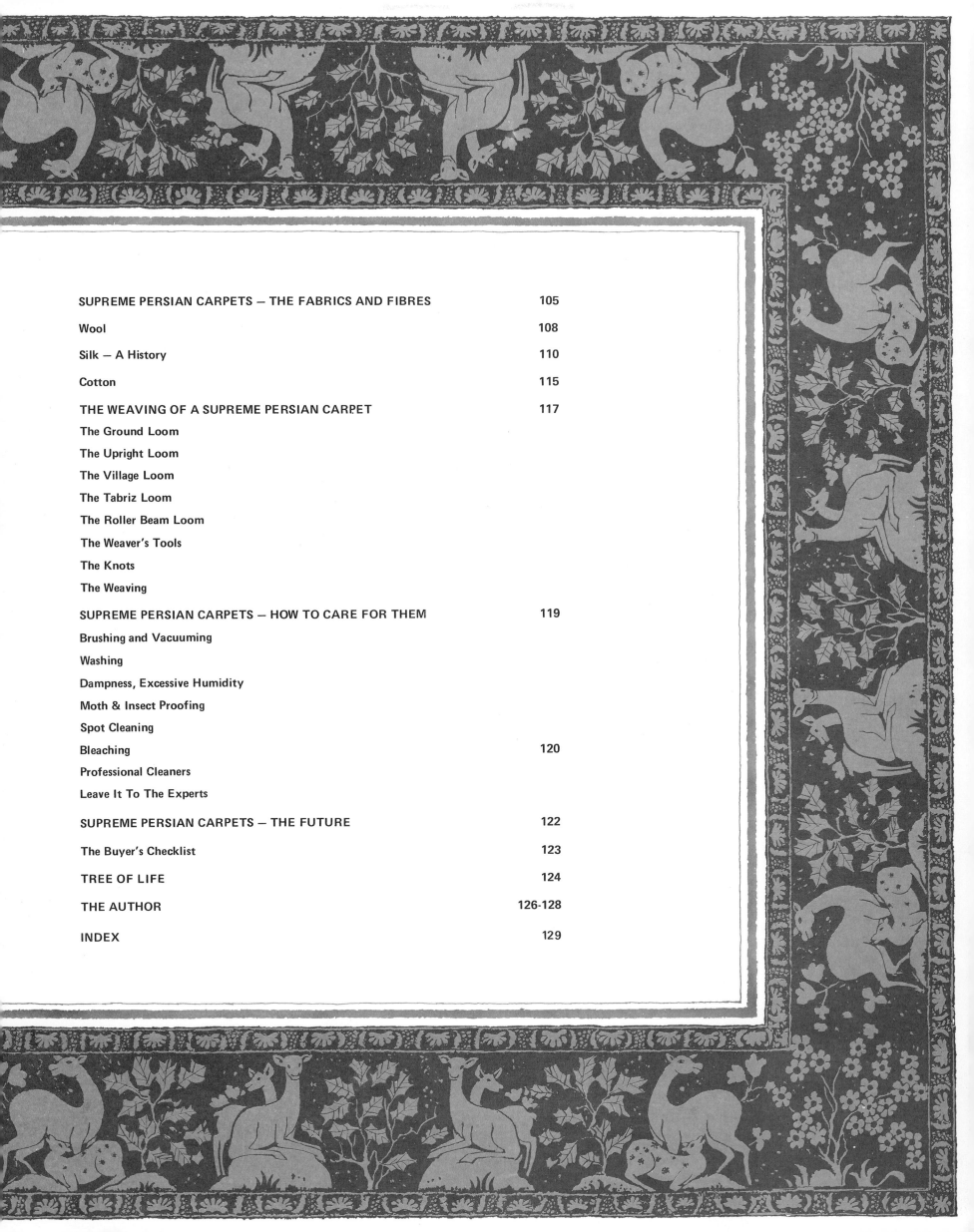

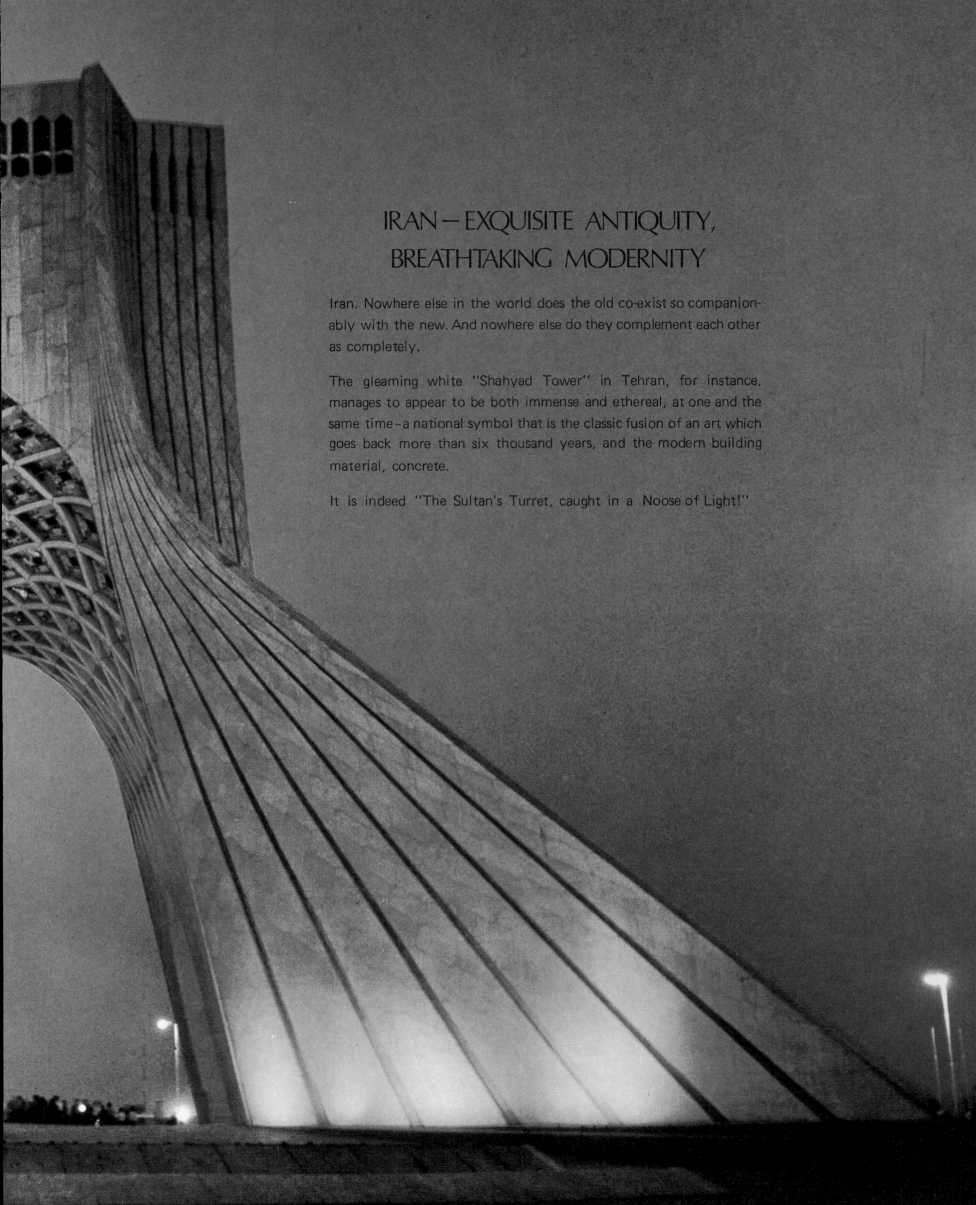

IRAN — EXQUISITE ANTIQUITY, BREATHTAKING MODERNITY

Iran. Nowhere else in the world does the old co-exist so companionably with the new. And nowhere else do they complement each other as completely.

The gleaming white "Shahyad Tower" in Tehran, for instance, manages to appear to be both immense and ethereal, at one and the same time—a national symbol that is the classic fusion of an art which goes back more than six thousand years, and the modern building material, concrete.

It is indeed "The Sultan's Turret, caught in a Noose of Light!"

THE OLD

It is fabulous, exquisite Persepolis. That quintessence of Kings. It is magnificent mosques, such as the Shah Mosque at Esfahan — a ceramic miracle. The cuniform inscriptions at Gabj-e Nameh, which bear silent witness to the grand titles and deeds of Darius and Xerxes. It is the Persian "Valley of the Kings", between Shiraz and Esfahan, where these great rulers lie buried, along with Artxerxes and Darius II. The holy city of Qum. Susa, where thirteen cities lie one upon the other, with the oldest dating back 4000 years. It is the bazaars of Esfahan where, turn a corner and, you are transported into the millenia. Nothing has changed. It is 'Qanats'. Underground ditches, sometimes 100 kilometres in length and 20 to 30 metres deep . . . a technique of establishing water that's at least 2500 years old — possibly older.

It is the "Towers of Silence" near Yezd. It is the Khandejan, south of Tabriz, with its troglodyte villages, largely unexplored. It is Persian Carpets — the history and aspirations of a people captured in a frieze of tapestry. It is everlasting. A spirit. An essence. It is the very dynamic that makes Iran great. And most of all, it is "fann" — a correct way of doing things. It is "fann" that is the link — the thread which weaves its rich mosaic through the fabric that is Iran.

THE NEW

It is black gold. Everflowing. Never ending oil. It is the wealth of Croesus. And more. It is incredible economic power. Huge dams. Water more precious than oil. Modern Industry that seemingly mushrooms overnight. It is bikini-clad girls on a resort beach. Magnificent deep-water ports. The flowering, where before desert sands held sway. It is the "Arya-Mehr" Stadium that can seat 100,000 people. And often does. It is the ever-increasing ribbons of superb highways and roads that bisect this huge (628,000 square miles) country. It is the twelve points of the "White Revolution" — the paving stones of modern Iran. It is 30,000, 000 people, united, with one voice, determined to lead the way into the 21st Century, yet not lose touch with the realities of today and yesterday. It is Universities. A desire, a thirst for knowledge. And where people cannot go to the schools of learning, the schools going to them. It is modern medicine. Hospitals. Stability in an unstable world. Acceptance of a destiny. It is a Monarchy that leads by example. The will of a nation not to be denied. And it is ultimately, "fann". Always "fann".

"Where thy carpet lies is thy house"

Persian Proverb

PERSIAN CARPETS—A BEGINNING

Years ago, in Persia and surrounding countries, a carpet was most times, the only item of furniture in a dwelling. Little wonder that Persian Carpets have evolved into such objects of beauty. A rich Persian house would display them as manifestations of wealth, while wandering tribes used them to insulate their tents from the ground, or to close off an entrance. The beautifully hued carpets no doubt enriched the lives of those tribes which led such an unremittingly severe and mostly austere life on the steppes and in the deserts of Asia.

As a document of tribal existence, Persian Carpets are unsurpassed. Their complex patterns and attention to detail related the visions that men had of the then world and were a reflection of the growth of the incredibly rich symbolism that permeated the very stuff of Persian life.

Today, the Persian Carpet serves much the same purpose. It is the ornament of mosques and palaces. And the talking point of many private dwellings. It is a reflection of taste that rejects the no-deposit, no-return society, for the concept of lasting artistic beauty combined with utility.

...A SHORT HISTORY

The oldest known carpet in existence is the one that was found at Pazyryk (Southern Siberia). It is said to have been manufactured sometime between the 5th and 1st Centuries, B.C.

Woollen carpets, the precursors of Persian Carpets were recorded during the reign of Cyrus the Great, but it is thought that these were made of woven cloth and not hand-knotted weaving. Unfortunately, no examples remain.

During the 10th Century around the **Fars** region and then, later on, in the 13th Century, around **Azarbaijan**, major Persian Carpet production took place. It has been suggested that the Arabs who conquered Persia during this period gave inspiration to the production of Persian Carpets, but this has never been substantiated. Indeed, what remaining evidence still exists, suggests that carpet production was a flourishing concern long before the Arabs embarked on their conquests.

For two hundred years, Persian Carpet production languished under the heel of the conquerors until the Safavid Dynasty—around 1500 A.D. — when the interlopers were shown the door, as it were. A period of greatness ensued. Shah Ismail, 1st ruler of the Safavid Dynasty, coopted the greatest painters of his kingdom to devise new patterns and expert weavers were called in to participate in this Persian Carpet 'Reformation'.

This was the beginning of the reputation that the region around Esfahan has maintained, even until today, as a major Persian Carpet production centre.

THE REIGN OF SHAH ABBAS THE GREAT
(1587-1629)

The next great period was during the reign of Shah Abbas the Great. And perhaps he, more than any other, helped elevate the Persian Carpet to the high art form that it still is. A skilled artist and craftsman, the Shah often wove cloth himself and it was through his singular efforts that carpet making flourished, first at **Joshaqan Quali,** (Joshaqan the carpet-town) about 65 miles south-west of **Esfahan** and then at **Kashan**.

The carpets woven during this period were larger than life, big in scale and somewhat grandiose in design — a reflection of Shah Abbas himself — containing as they did, great palmettes, huge leaves, flower-strewn meadows and sometimes, animals. The carpets, used as wall hangings, table cloths and floor coverings, were enriched with threads of silk, gold-covered silver and silver. The secret of this silk and silver thread embellishment, always a jealously guarded secret, went to the grave with thousands of Esfahanis, during the Afghan invasion, near the end of the 17th Century. Fortunately, a number of the some 2000 carpets woven during this period survived. They are universally recognised as unparalleled works of art and experts cannot even place them in order of merit, so great is the craftsmanship.

MODERN CARPET MANUFACTURE

Then followed some 200 years of the Persian equivalent of the ' Dark Ages'. It wasn't until the early 19th Century that a further 'Reformation' occurred. Under the patronage of the rich merchant-classes of Tehran, Tabriz and Kirman, old techniques and crafts were resurrected. So successful were these efforts, that carpet making became Persia's major industry and export earner. During the next 20 years or so, new techniques were adopted and the industry burgeoned.

Unfortunately, the Great War interfered with this ' Reformation ': However, thanks to the foresight of Reza Shah the Great, the NATIONAL CARPET COMPANY was established. The Company set up workshops in all provinces and actively contributed to the creation of new designs, which helped Persian Carpet manufacture survive this new setback.

After World War I, Persian Carpet production continued to flourish, until today, when it faces perhaps its most severe test yet. With modern industry absorbing the labour force as it becomes available and also with the relatively high wages that Modern Industry offers, Persian Carpet· production has almost ceased. Only Government intervention and the setting up of subsidized "Craft" centres has prevented it dying out altogether.

THE PEOPLES OF IRAN

THE KURD
These warrior farmers and herdsmen have inhabited the mountains of Kurdistan (North Western Iran) for many centuries.

THE LUR
These basically nomadic people, who inhabit the mountain areas of North Western Iran with several other tribes, have great flocks of sheep and herds of goats, both of which fleeces are used in Persian Carpet making.

THE QASHQAI
Yet another nomadic tribe, South Western Iran, the Qashqai spend their time herding massive numbers of sheep from winter pastures to the fertile Iranian highlands and back again.

THE BALUCHI
A rich tribe, with large herds of camels, sheep and goats, the Baluchi live a nomadic existence on the borders of Iran, Pakistan and Afghanistan.

TABRIZ
ARDEBAIL
MARAGHEH
RASHT
ZANJAN
KHIVA
YAMOOD
GORGAN
HARITZ
BIJAR
TEHRAN
SENNEH
KASHAN
HAMADAN
QOM
KERMANSHAH
JOSHAQAN

IRAN (PERSIA)

ISFAHAN
NAIN
YEZD
AHVAZ
KHURRAMSHAR
ABADEH
KERMAN
ABADAN
SHIRAZ

IRAN-HOME OF SUPREME PERSIAN CARPETS

THE PERSIANS
It is from the Persians that Iran has most of its cultural impetus, as they are artisans of the first order, with traditions that reach back 3000 years.

THE TAJIK
The Tajik trace their origins back to the ancient Persians of South Western Afghanistan. They grow the fine cotton which is used in the weaving process.

THE PASHTUN
Spilling over from modern day Afghanistan, where in fact a Pashtun King presently rules, the Pashtun were immortalised by Ripling as the Parthans.

THE HAZARA
The Mongol influence is still strong amongst this remote tribe, who tend to live in the high valleys of Afghanistan.

THE TURKOMAN
Famed for the Karakul sheep, better known as Persian Lamb, the Turkomans are nomads of North Eastern Iran. Turkoman women weave the superb Bokhara carpets.

SAMARKAND

KASGAR

MASHHAD · YARKAND

MIZERASHERIEF

BIRJAND

TALOQAN

MEYMANEH

BASHIRE

JALALABAD

KABUL

AFGHANISTAN

QANDAHAR

SUPREME PERSIAN CARPETS—
QUALITY AND STATUS CHARTS

KASHAN • QUM
ESFAHAN • NAHEEN
JOSHAGAN • TABRIZ • SAROUKE • SENNEH/FERAGHAN
KERMANSHAH • BAHKTIARI • HERIZ • MASHHAD • BIRJAND
KIRMAN • AFSHAR • YEZD • SARABAND • NIRIS • BIJAR • ABADEH • SHIRAJE

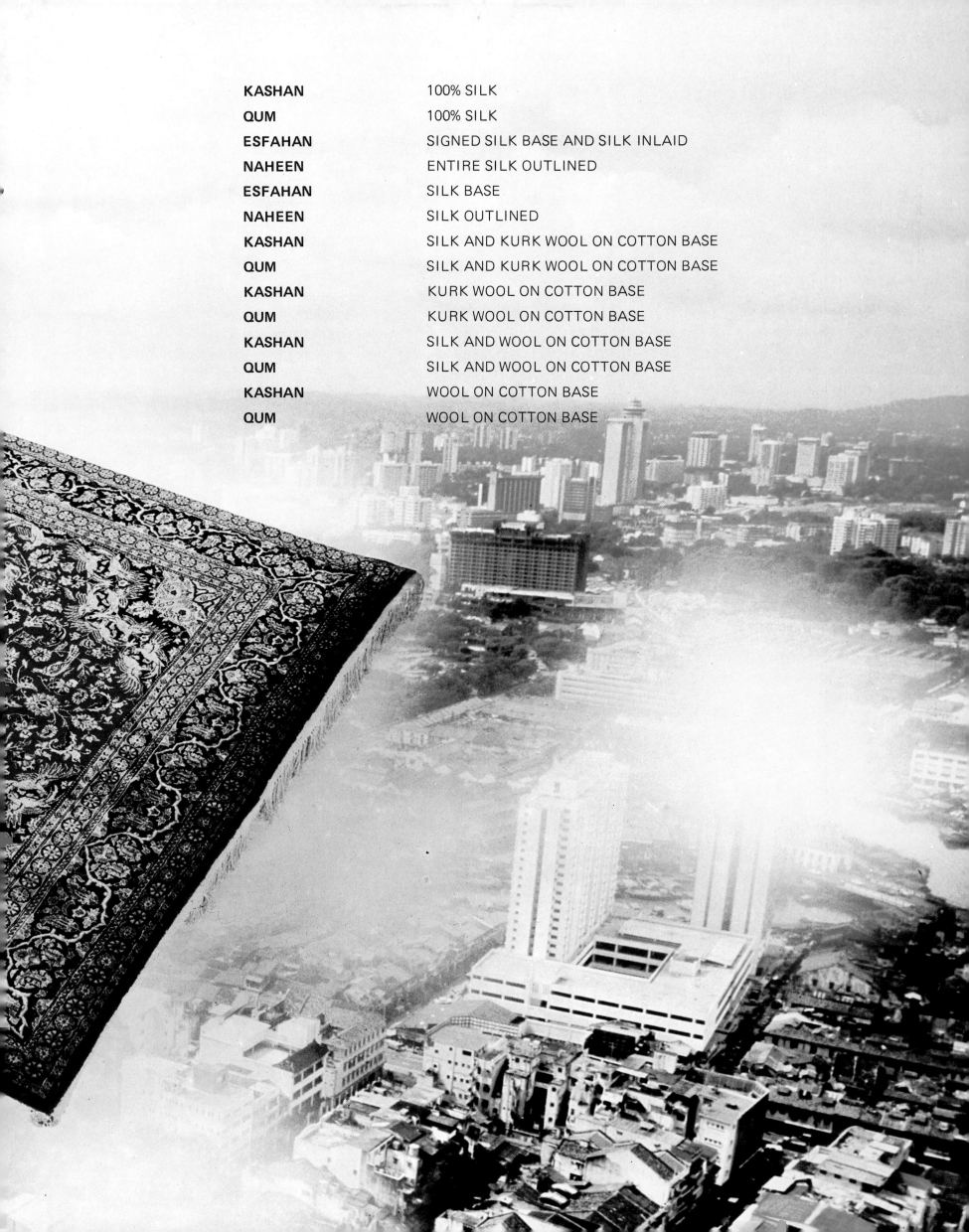

KASHAN	100% SILK
QUM	100% SILK
ESFAHAN	SIGNED SILK BASE AND SILK INLAID
NAHEEN	ENTIRE SILK OUTLINED
ESFAHAN	SILK BASE
NAHEEN	SILK OUTLINED
KASHAN	SILK AND KURK WOOL ON COTTON BASE
QUM	SILK AND KURK WOOL ON COTTON BASE
KASHAN	KURK WOOL ON COTTON BASE
QUM	KURK WOOL ON COTTON BASE
KASHAN	SILK AND WOOL ON COTTON BASE
QUM	SILK AND WOOL ON COTTON BASE
KASHAN	WOOL ON COTTON BASE
QUM	WOOL ON COTTON BASE

"For lust of knowing what should not be known,
We take the Golden Road to Samarkand . . ."

J.E. Flecker

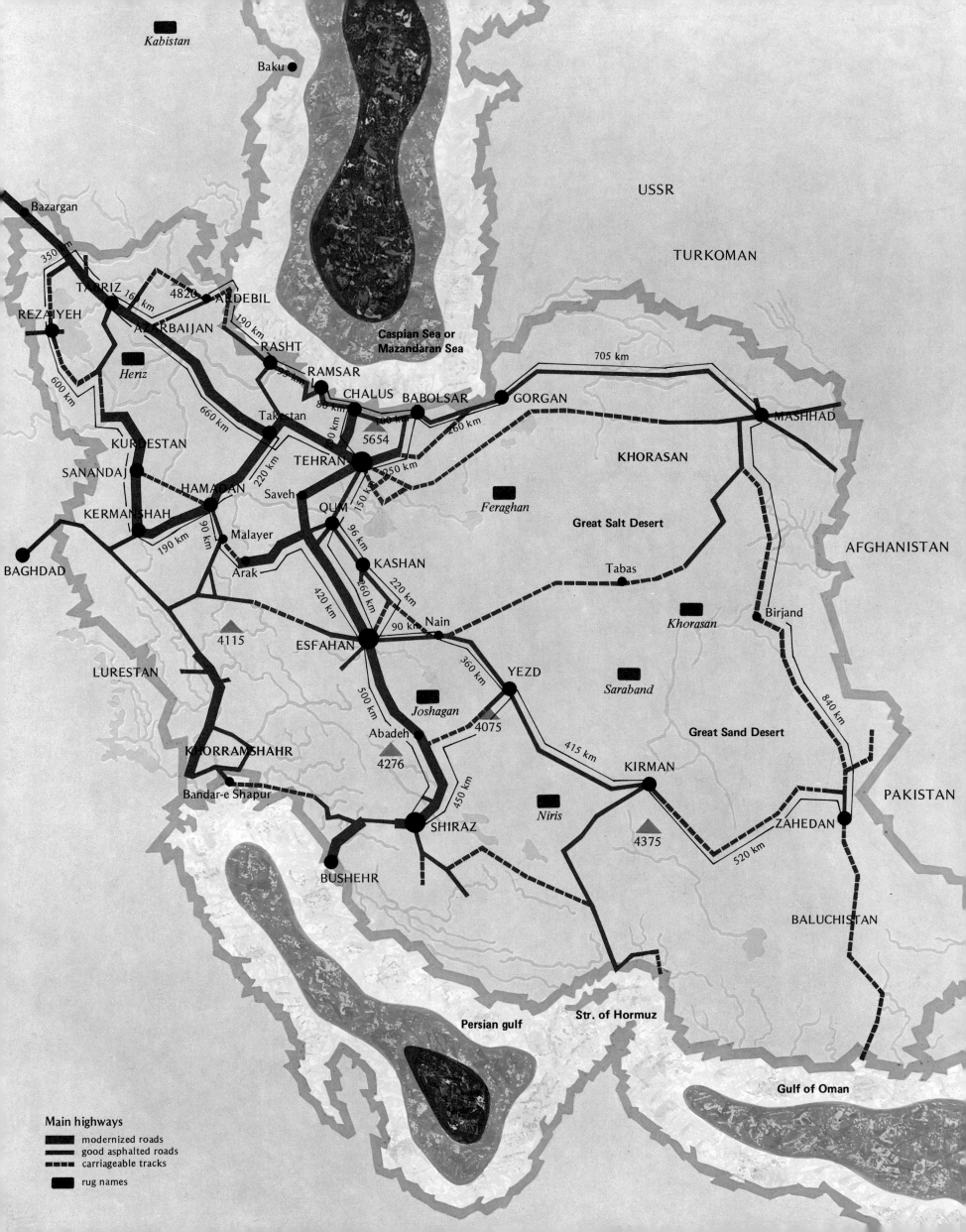

Kabistan

Baku

USSR

TURKOMAN

Bazargan

350 km

TABRIZ 160 km 4820 ARDEBIL

REZAIYEH

AZERBAIJAN

190 km

RASHT

600 km

Henz

660 km

RAMSAR

55 km

CHALUS

80 km

BABOLSAR

100 km

GORGAN

705 km

MASHHAD

Caspian Sea or
Mazandaran Sea

260 km

Takestan

200 km

TEHRAN

5654

KHORASAN

KURDESTAN

SANANDAJ

HAMADAN

220 km

Saveh

250 km

150 km

Feraghan

Great Salt Desert

KERMANSHAH

190 km 90 km

Malayer

QUM

96 km

AFGHANISTAN

BAGHDAD

Arak

420 km 260 km

KASHAN

220 km

Tabas

Khorasan

Birjand

4115

90 km Nain

ESFAHAN

YEZD

840 km

LURESTAN

360 km

Saraband

500 km

Joshagan

4075

KHORRAMSHAHR

Abadeh

415 km

4276

KIRMAN

Great Sand Desert

Bandar-e Shapur

450 km

Niris

4375

ZAHEDAN

PAKISTAN

SHIRAZ

520 km

BUSHEHR

BALUCHISTAN

Persian gulf

Str. of Hormuz

Gulf of Oman

Main highways

▬▬▬ modernized roads

▬▬▬ good asphalted roads

▬ ▬ ▬ carriageable tracks

■ rug names

TEHRAN

This is a city which continually surprises—an endless array of perfectly straight avenues and boulevards which cross each other at right angles and at each intersection, a fountain, a monument that is a work of art, or, a beautifully worked flower garden.

More than three million people live here and with the ever increasing population has come modernity. Towering skyscrapers seemingly mushroom overnight. New roads have been built to link the far-flung suburbs, which are up to a mile above sea level in places. Shopping malls have also grown apace. And government has not stood still either—public buildings and government departments have been continually expanded to meet the public demand.

Perhaps the focal point of Tehran is the immense yet remarkably beautiful Shahyad Tower. It is a superb national monument which reflects the new spirit of Iran and it also houses one of the finest museums in the world. As well, the visitor is entertained to an incredible audio-visual display on the creation of the world and Iran.

Tehran is also pleasant to be in: It has a dry, crisp climate; a clear blue sky; mountain views; cool evenings; and an inpressive number of superbly manicured parks and gardens, where flowers dazzle with their colours—all year round. Tehran abounds in things for the visitor to see. The Golestan Palace, for instance. Its ancient splendour was revived for the coronation ceremony of the Shah and Shahbanou in 1967 and is still used for formal State occasions. However, its grounds are open to all visitors who may wish to stroll and explore in this garden of delight. Also not to be missed is the Takht-e-Tavous or "Peacock Throne". Symbol of royalty, it is a square divan, encrusted with precious gems.

THE CARPET BAZAAR. More than 10 kilometres of covered streets make up the carpet bazaar, although an extraordinary number of other goods are sold there also. Dealers are grouped by speciality and whole streets, or quarters, are devoted to each enterprise. For the inhabitants, the bazzar is their world, which they very rarely leave. That the carpet bazaar is important is reflected in the fact that fully two-thirds of all Persian Carpets sold, are sold here.

Unfortunately, Tehran is no longer a weaving centre, but those Tehran carpets which survive, notably of the Portico and Panel designs, with a Tree-of-Life motif prominent, suggest a quality comparable with Kashan, Kirman and Esfahan. The prevailing colours stand out because of the softness and beauty of the vegetable dye hues, while the wide, distinctive borders are similar in flavour to those carpets from Joshaghan.

QUM

About 150 km south of Tehran, along a modern highway, lies Qum — one of the most important holy towns in Iran. It is known as the 'Holy City' to those of the Shi'ite belief. Activities in Qum are mainly centred on what is known as the 'Sanctuary' — a place of high walls and forbiddingly big portals. The golden dome and minarets of the 'Sanctuary' dominate the skyline from every part of the city and nowhere are they seen to better advantage than · from the terraces of a nearby hotel — comfortable enough, but not of the five-star variety.

Qum has a thriving weaving industry, which has been mostly influenced by the merchants of Kashan. Most rugs woven here are on a cream background and the designs, while repetitive, tend to be more eclectic than other centres — borrowing as they do, from any number of patterns. That notwithstanding, there is a quite discernible Qum-cum-Kashan style, centred on the Turkish, or double knot.

Supreme Persian Carpets
By H. K. Zephyr Amir

ESFAHAN

Of this city, some 490 km south of Tehran (the newly widened highway is excellent) it has been said, "Esfahan is half the world". And when one sees its incredible buildings, mosques, and mosaics, one recognises the sophistication and magnificence that was and still is, the Persian civilization. Here is sight upon sight for the traveller. A feast of beauty that would suffice the gourmet. One needs a week to see the best of it and then, a week is not long enough.

The bridges, the Royal Square, the Shah Abbas Mosque and a dozen other mosques, the palaces, the Shaking Minarets, the oasis, the gardens, the pigeon houses, the giant, 50-metre-high minarets, the Armenian quarter, and the river—always the river. The senses are stunned by it all.

There is a proverb which says: "Who comes to Esfahan cannot fall ill, who comes there ill will see his health restored". Like a good white wine, the air is dry, yet subtle. There are temperature extremes, but in Spring, the weather becomes gentle and balmy. The gardens and surrounds are laden with flowers and all is right with the world. It was at Esfahan that the great Shah Abbas founded a dynasty of Persian Carpet design that has stayed constant to this day. From here, the Shah Abbas influence has spread all over Iran.

Rich in floral and animal decoration of the finest type, with large palmettes and rich patternings, connected by vines, serrated leaves and various tree forms, Esfahan Carpets have to be seen to be believed. The Herati pattern is shown at its most elaborate, while colours that almost overpower are blues, greens, deep crimsons and deep wine colours known as Esfahan red. The field colours are generally of deep red or blue on a silk base.

KASHAN

250 km south of the Capital lies Kashan, famous for pottery and glazed tiles, as well as its successful carpet industry. Situated on the edge of the Great Desert, its greenery contrasts sharply with the surrounding parched landscape. It is here that the visitor can see a system of qanats, or water canals, in working order. Here, fountains abound in private houses, adding the finishing touches to already picturesque gardens.

Kashan is the centre of the silk rug industry in Iran and it is believed that the famous Ardebil carpet was woven here, although no-one can say for sure. As a class, Kashan silks are the best silk rugs made. Two designs predominate, namely the medallion-and-corner type with covered grounds and the Shah Abbas, or floral type with many connecting vines. The prevailing colours tend to be dark blues, reds, greens, rose, turquoise, a deep wine colour and ivory. The touchstone of most Kashan carpets is the Mustofi border — a rose intersected by leaves and repeated all round the carpet. A phenomenon among antique Kashan carpets are a number of old "Hunting Carpets", with elaborate detail work, showing hunters and dogs pursuing animals of the chase, among forest glades. The master weavers of Kashan are said to be the pioneers of the Persian Carpet weaving industry.

NAIN

Half-way between Esfahan and Yezd and about 500 km from Tehran, this small but pretty town is also worth a stop for more than its carpets — namely, three mosques. Their cupolas are superb examples of an architectural style that has the deepest religious connotations. One of them, the Nain mosque, was built at the very dawn of Islam and is the most ancient in all of Iran. It was known to have been partially rebuilt in 960 A.D.

Nain carpets have a reputation second-to-none for the closeness of their weave. This is no doubt due to the fine weaving techniques that were developed when textiles and tapestries were produced in the town in great quantity.

The carpets woven in Nain, are known as Naheens and are usually silk-outlined to give an extra dimension to the patternings. Basic designs include medallions repeated on a floral field with a floral border, somewhat reminiscent of Esfahani patterns. The carpets, because of the weaving, are extremely durable and are the stuff that family heirlooms are made of — to be passed down from generation to generation.

YEZD

Something of a side trip is necessary to travel to this ancient city, about 340 km south-east of Esfahan. It is a true desert city, with a lively economy — carpet manufacture, tin- and copper-smithing and textile weaving being the mainstays. Yezd has an architecture unlike any other Iranian town. This perhaps being an influence of the Zoroastrians who settled in the region. The city has several ' Fire Temples ' on its outskirts, which can only be viewed from the outside. Also worth taking a trip for, are the imposing ' Towers of Silence ' which again can only be viewed from without.

The predominant design used in Yezd carpets is that of the Herati, with a special variation — the leaves of the design are especially long. Generally, wide turtle borders are employed, reflecting both Kirman and Tabrizi influences. The Persian knot is used almost exclusively, which makes for a very fine quality weave. The Turkish knot is used for the heavier quality rugs. Colours tend towards red, old browns, tans, blues and ivory. Yezd rugs are quite often found in mosques, hence the great demand for them.

JOSHAGAN

For nearly three hundred years, this poor village and surrounding districts 150 km south-west of Esfahan, has produced carpets which rival the best that Kashan can offer. And for this reason, if no other, the traveller should take the side-trip to view them.

No matter the age of a Joshagan carpet, the design is always the same—rectilinear. There is never a curved line in a Joshagan weave, whether or not a central medallion has been used. Typically, a type of scroll is carried throughout the margin of the field and a common design is a series of crosses and eight-pointed stars. Colours are generally soft and the ground is usually red or blue. The carpets themselves are usually large and they sometimes resemble the Saraband, although silk is never used by the Joshagani weavers.

ABADEH

A little over half-way between Esfahan and Shiraz — about 300 km south of Esfahan, it serves as a welcome stop-over for travellers — lies this small and pretty market town.

That it no longer serves as a carpet-producing centre is unfortunate, because those examples which remain give some indication that here was a fine quality product. However, perhaps its present function — that of serving as a gathering point for carpets woven in the surrounding hamlets and countryside — makes amends.

KIRMAN

This provincial capital, 590 km south-west of Tehran is the carpet centre of southern Kurdistan. Not surprisingly, one would meet a large number of Kurds in the district — a one-time fierce warrior breed who are unfailingly polite and sociable to visitors.

3 km north of Kirman is an incredible vestige of the 3rd Century A.D — the Taq-e Bostan. A group of rock sculptures, including kings, courtiers, all manner of animals and horsemen, in a pleasing and harmonious composition. For the past few generations Kirman has been producing a richer variety of magnificent designs in rugs, than the rest of Iran put together. The carpets are noted for their long pile and the central medallion or Classic Floral fields and floral borders. Borders vary from three to five stripes and colours in soft shades of pinks, greens, or blues on a field of old ivory, are in the majority.

SHIRAZ

From the airport to the city runs an unbroken line of rose gardens, eight kilometres long. Little wonder Shiraz is known as the "City of roses, wine and poets".

This capital city of Fars Province, one of the five major provinces of Iran, is the cradle of the Persian monarchy. Cyrus the Great was born here. And carpets were reportedly woven here more than 1000 years ago.

Situated 500 km south of Esfahan, Shiraz is rapidly becoming a "must-see" for all visitors to Iran. A world-famous art festival is held here annually and is not the least of its attractions. Nearby, along a modern highway, lies fabled Persepolis, with all its magnificent ruins and artefacts, just waiting to entrance the visitor and to help him lose himself in antiquity.

The city has a pleasant climate, very mild in winter and not too hot in summer. Which might explain why it has always had a reputation for intellectuals and poets — an equitable climate in a city of long, wide shady avenues and parks with splendid trees, goes a long way to help serious contemplation.

Generally, carpets of the Farsi are tribal and because of this are usually of a geometrical design — pole medallions being frequently incorporated. As a rule, animal motifs feature strongly and the pear pattern is also common. Colours that prevail are usually rich wine colours, autumnal shades, deep, rich blues, reds, yellows, greens; dark blue fields are also a feature. Occasionally a barber-pole stripe is employed as a border design.

Farsi rugs are normally all-wool, which has led them to be overlooked by carpet buyers. However, there is nothing wrong with the Fars quality and it is more than likely you will pick up a genuine bargain in carpets of this region, as Shirage all-wool rugs are renowned tribal rugs of southern Iran. Incidentally, the newly widened highway makes driving from Esfahan to Shiraz a pleasure.

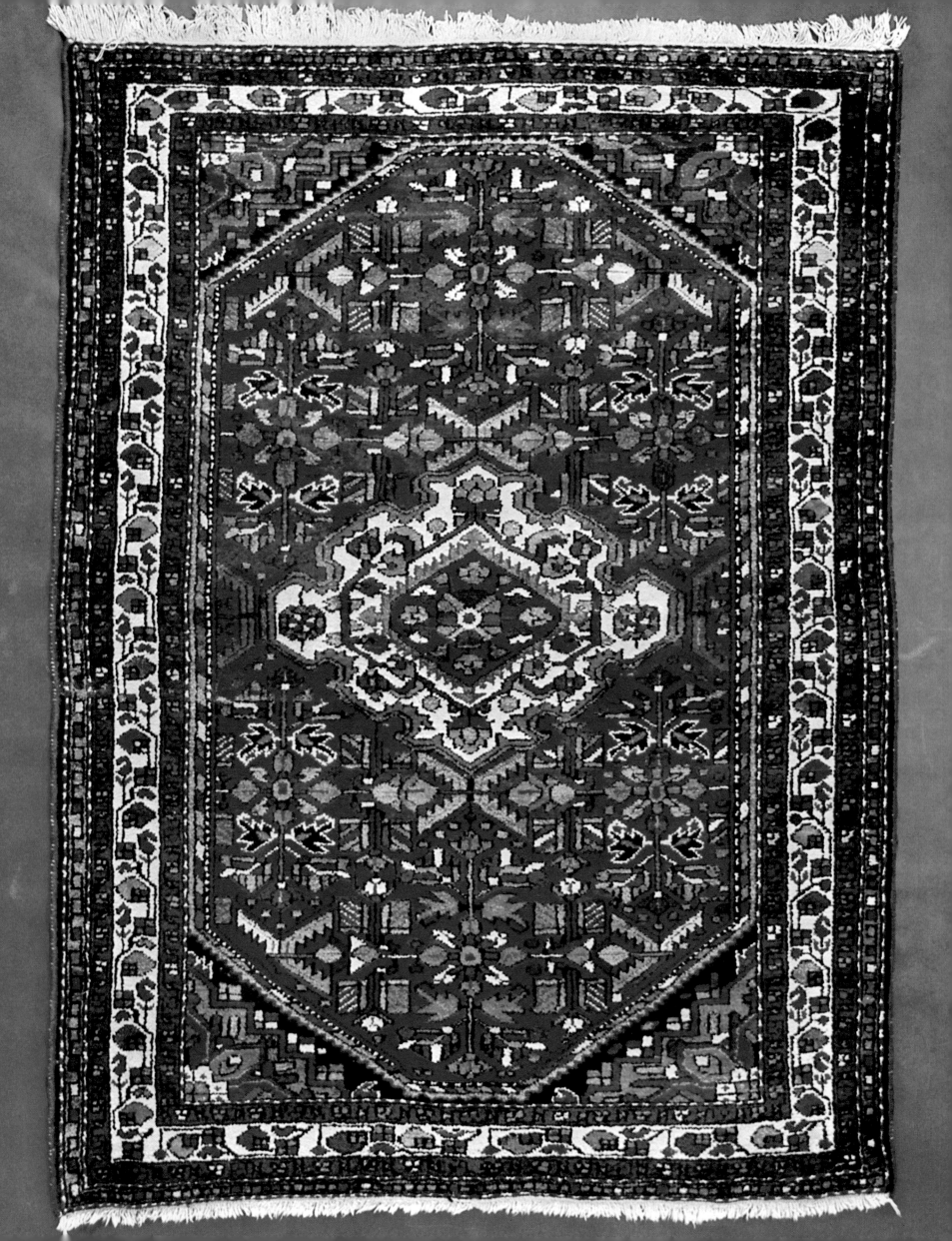

HAMADAN

400 km north-west of the Capital, lies Hamadan, which main claim to fame is that it is built on the site of the ancient city of the same name — the capital city of the Medes before they formed a union with the Persians.

Perhaps the most significant sights in this region are: the cuniform inscriptions at Ganj-e Nameh, which extoll the virtues and various titles of Darius and Xerxes; the Mongol Towers, remnants of the 12th Century — above the tomb of Avicenna; and a Jewish Mausoleum reputed to contain the tombs of Esther and Mordecai. Jews come from all over the Middle East on pilgrimages to Hamadan.

The tradition of carpet weaving here goes back many years and Hamadan is renowned for its inexpensive, quality rugs — which is not surprising, for it also has a reputation as one of the foremost weaving centres of Iran. Most of the rugs produced here are tribal, and are named after the particular villages from whence they come. There is a large Armenian population and the Turkish knot predominates.

The pole medallion is almost universal, while the field is usually filled with floral designs, or a unique grape-vine design or trellis arrangement. Colours mostly used include; natural camel-hair brown, with soft, delicate reds, pinks, blues and greens.

Malayer: While in the Hamadan region, this town cannot be regarded as one of the Hamadan villages as the designs are closer to those of Arak—pure Persian—even though the Turkish knot is employed.

KURDISTAN

North-west of Tehran, close to the Turkish and Iraqi borders, lies Persian Kurdistan. To get there, the visitor has to travel through mountainous country—sometimes on little better than dirt tracks. There is little for the visitor in terms of antiquities, or architectural grandeur, but one can be sure of a warm welcome in the small villages. However, care should be taken not to fall into the hands of the occasional bandit gangs which raid across the border.

The weaving tribes of Persian Kurdistan excel in their efforts and four weaves stand out:

a) **Senneh:** This town, about 100 miles from Hamadan produces rugs that have a refinement of texture and originality that is unsurpassed by any other Persian weave. They are also unique and unmistakable, for no other Persian rug resembles them. The-Flower-and-Bird, the Gol Mohammedi (pink roses on a blue field) and the Vekilli (variegated lozenges on the field with small repetitive patterns in the borders) are just some of the designs that have made Senneh famous.

b) **Bijar:** The Bijar carpet from the town of the same name is a distant relative to the Turkish Ushak and the Herati design holds sway in the patternings. Normally, a centre medallion without corner pieces also manifests itself. Far from being a drawback, the few and simple designs tend to enhance the quality of the weave—not detract from it.

c) **Kurdish Tribal Rugs:** These rugs are woven within a 50-mile radius of a village named Qurveh. The designs are tribal and quite distinct from the mainstream of Persian Carpet patternings.

d) **Arak:** This town, to the south-west of Tehran is one of the four most important weaving centres of Iran. Persian carpets available from this region are cheap in the extreme, yet the quality is medium to fine. Designs are almost always derivatives of the classic Herati, Gol Henai, Mina Khani, Harshang, Shah Abbas and Joshagani designs.

ARDEBAIL

260 km east of Tabriz lies Ardebail —a coastal town on the Caspian Sea. Approaching it, from either Tabriz or Chalus, the visitor is almost overwhelmed by the succession of superb landscapes which unfold. And yet, the town itself is surrounded by endless expanses of sheep-grazing land. Sheep are the basic of the economy here. In the elongated Bazaar, the visitor will find astrakhan hats, caps and bonnets by the score. The visitor will also find a very warm welcome from the unaffected people of the region.

In the town itself, the visitor will find an unusual monument—a 8-metre high round tower. Built in the 14th Century, it has a blue geometrical design on a brick background which is astonishingly modern. The monument overlooks two tombs, which surrounds take the form of finely engraved wood panels with incredibly delicate ivory and rare metal inlays.

The town itself no longer produces carpets, for they are woven in the surrounding villages. The carpets are almost invariably woven in the lozenge pattern and are always aesthetically pleasing. Blue, greens, deep reds and darker natural wool colours tend to stand out.

MASHHAD

The holy city of Iran, this beautiful spot, lying close to the borders of the U.S.S.R. and Afghanistan, is some 1275 km north-east of Tehran.

The sacred enclosure is dominated by turquoise blue and beaten gold pagolas. Non-Moslems are not allowed through the Astane Ghods (the Sacred Threshold) and even from a distance, observation should be discreet. It is here that Shi'ite Islam's most revered saint lies buried— Ali Reza, the Eighth Imam. The visitor will be fascinated by the black-clad faithful, as they move in mournful processions, tolling their prayer beads.

The museum has much to offer the visitor also, including many prayer carpets with gold and silver threads, beautifully engraved string-courses and several very rare Korans. The railway station also deserves attention. It is a superb example of the work of the French architect, Fernand Pouillon.

One side trip that is a must, is to the town of Neyshabur, 130 km west of Mashhad. Here are the tombs of the great Persian poets, Omar Khayyam and Sheikh-e Attar, and of Mahrug, prophet of Islam. The tombs are surrounded by magnificent gardens, where the visitor can wile away the hours. One should also visit the turquoise-cutting workshops while in the town.

The predominant carpet designs from Mashhad are Herati, medallion centres with matching corners, and pear. Animist designs are also sometimes seen. Colours include a rich magenta, soft shades of blue, green, pink and ivory. Cochineal is used in preference to madder for the production of reds.

SAROUKE

Some 200 km north-west of Tehran, on the old road to Hamadan south of Arak, this small, picturesque village produces some beautiful carpets and not much else.

The designs are marked by the fact that there is always a medallion, with freely introduced flower patterns — on occasion, almost grotesque floral shapes. The borders are generally Herati and sometimes the Shah Abbas. Prevailing colours include dark seal browns, or greens and reds, generally on a field of ivory, blue or red.

TABRIZ

A large city, with more than 500,000 inhabitants, Tabriz is the second city of Iran. It lies astride an old caravan route, some 650 km north-west of Tehran and was founded in the 7th Century.

The city itself is architecturally unimpressive, but the Blue Mosque is worth a visit, for the splendid beauty of its enamelled compositions, with all manner of blues ranging from turquoise to ultramarines. The College of Miniature Paintings also is worth putting on your list. One feature you'll readily notice is the family picnics that are so popular among the Tabrizi, especially in the 'Golestan', or Rose Garden — a large park with wide expanses of water and a superb central pavillion. In the Bazaar, you'll find Armenians, Turkomans and Kurds working side-by-side in stalls piled high with all manner of leather goods, fabrics and tin objects.

For the adventurous, a visit to the Khandejah region, south of Tabriz, will reward with the sight of troglodyte villages — one of the few examples of underground dwellings in the world today. This part of Iran is largely uncharted and travellers must exercise common sense. A day side-trip towards the Turkish Frontier to the church of St. Thaddeus is also worthwhile. This astonishing fortified Christian monastary was built during the 11th to the 14th Centuries. Once a year, in early July, Armenians meet here for a colourful pastoral celebration.

Tabriz and surrounding areas, such as Heriz, take pride of place in Persian Carpet weaving. It is Tabriz that we have to thank for the medallion-and-corners design, which emanated in the region. It is said that the weavers here, are the fastest in all Iran and that the best of them can tie 15,000 knots a day — using the Persian single knot at that!

Designs are nearly always the medallion with field covered with intricate floral designs. Frequently, verses from the Koran or by Persian poets will be found woven in the borders. Tree-of-Life patterns are also frequent and a heart-shaped lamp often hangs from the niche in prayer rugs. Along with the Kirman, the Tabriz shares the reputation of having the most graceful floral designs. They are purely Persian and have suffered little from outside influence. A tendency to curve at the edges is not a negative among these rugs, as it is a sign of extremely close weaving. Colours tend towards bright blues, reds and browns, while ivory is a regular field colour.

THE HERIZ: 40 miles due south-east of Tabriz, lies the village and the area of Heriz — one of the most interesting weaving areas of Iran. The population is almost exclusively Turkish and it is here that the remarkable carpets known as Gorevans are woven. So full of character, these rugs are a possession to be prized.

There is a great prevalence of Mongolian influence in their designs, which are usually straight-line copies of curved-line patterns. Colours of blue, red, and green in all their shades; also brown, old ivory, terra cotta and yellow, are seen to predominate. Gorevans are excellent wearing carpets.

The Serapi: These rugs are named after a village and are similar to the Gorevan. They are the finest of the Heriz district rugs, usually with more detail in design than others. Colours are similar also to the Gorevan, but are usually brighter.

The Bakhshis: Also named after a village, these rugs are rare and among the most desirable of the region's carpets. Designs are similar to Gorevans, with a characteristic angular ornamentation. Shah Abbas, Herati and Sadar designs are frequently used. Colours are also similar to others in the region, with a smattering of old rose used in the field.

CHALUS

Almost due north of Tehran, about 200 km , lies the Caspian Sea resort town of Chalus—a resort with a difference, encompassing forests, incredible greenery and mountain views. There is a beautiful hinterland and the visitor should not hesitate to take one of the small roads or tracks that lead to small, attractive rural villages, for here is a rustic charm found nowhere else in Iran.

Today, Chalus is the centre of the Caucasian Carpet trade, where the rugs from south-eastern and south-western parts of the Caspian Sea coast are marketed.

The Caucasian Carpets, which are mostly woven by people of Armenian extraction are similar in design and colouring to those of ancient Assyria and Babylon. The main classifications are:

DAGHESTAN. Fine, closely woven with diagonal ornamentation of both border and field. The centre is never plain and floral forms are seldom used. The Greek Cross is almost omnipresent.

DERBEND. Very good weave with a purely geometric design. The latch hook and eight-pointed stars are the most common devices. The field usually consists of a repetition of designs in alternate colours.

KABISTAN. Closely woven and usually floral designs with interconnecting meander lines. Small broadcast flowers, tarantulas, swastikas, S-forms, diamonds, stars, birds and animals. are most common. The carnation in profile is the most common border.

CHICHI. Usually well woven but looser than some. Designs are hard to tabulate, usually a mixture of Caucasian and Persian designs repeated over a field in a trellis form. Diamond-shaped figures, rosettes, trefoils and tarantula are evident . Colours are usually dark.

LESGHIAN. This name applies to so many nomadic fabrics that the term has little meaning. However, the designs are distinctly Caucasian and extremely simple, being mainly mosaics tempered by floral forms.

TCHERKESS. Finely woven and very rare. Designs are eclectic but the field is almost always filled with the sun-burst or palace design.

SHIRVAN. Very fine and perhaps the best known of the modern Caucasians. Designs are similar to those of Daghestans and Kabistan. Borders often have the scorpion and wine glass motifs. Colours that prevail are quiet hues of red, blue, yellow and salmon, with considerable use made of fine white wool.

BAKU. Generally closely woven and well tied, with the large pear pattern most common. Frequently, a central medallion with corners to match is used. One of the characteristics of the Baku is a thin streak of camel's hair thrown across one end.

SHEMAKHA. Woven in the same primitive fashion as of old, it is the only pileless Oriental rug besides the Khilim. All designs are outlined in black and the Mongolian influence is perceptible. Animals are frequently portrayed.

TIFLIS. Competently woven with designs that usually take the form of hexagonal pears, trees, etc.

KUTAIS. Fine carpets with pear motifs and tree forms. The field is frequently divided by a number of bands which run parallel to the sides and which carry vine designs. Colours include blue, red and white.

KARABAGH. Coarsely woven with floral designs. Sometimes black and tan spots on the field suggest leopard's skin. Very artistic.

GENGHIS. Somewhat coarsely woven with geometrical designs. The pear is frequently employed, usually in alternate rows of red and blue. Birds and animals are also used.

SHUSHA. Similar in quality and design to the Karabagh but very rare because of limited quantities made.

KAZAK. Made by Cossak Nomads, these are much sought after for their fine weave. Bold geometrical designs are characteristic with tarantulas, diamonds, palms, animals and human beings profusely portrayed. Colours are rather bright shades of red, green, yellow, with ivory and white. The Greek Cross is almost always present in the border and the Russian Coat of Arms is also common.

GORGAN

The gateway to the great Persian Steppe—the birthplace of Turkoman or Bokhara Carpets—is Gorgan. It lies close to the Russo-Iranian border about 550 km north-east of Tehran.

There are two routes to Gorgan, both about the same in distance from the Capital. The first is by way of Karaj then on to Chalus—the Caucasian rug centre. Then, a pleasant drive along the shores of the Caspian Sea takes you to Behshahr and through the small town of Sari. From here to Gorgan is flat and somewhat uninteresting, however, as one approaches Gorgan, farming country prevails. The second and more interesting way, is across the mountains via the picturesque town of Abali, then down to Sari, thence to Gorgan.

Even though the main centre of production of Bokhara Carpets is Turkoman, in Russian-dominated Turkestan, it is possible to obtain a representative selection of Bokharas in Gorgan. There are at least eleven different Bokhara Carpet-weaving regions which encompass an enormous area, including Beluchistan, Afghanistan, U.S.S.R.-Turkestan and a large part of northern and north-west Iran.

There is a commonality of colours and design in Bokharas and usually, the predominant background colour is a deep red, with geometrical patterns repeated in dark blue, maroon, cream, black, cream and tan, sometimes even white

The major Bokhara Classifications are:

	KHIVA BOKHARA
	YAMUD BOKHARA
	TEKKE BOHARA (GUZELLE)
	AFGHAN BOKHARA
WESTERN TURKESTAN	BESHIR BOKHARA
	KIRGHIS
TURKOMAN	ERSARI
	SAMARKAND
EASTERN TURKESTAN	KASHGAR
	YARKAND
(IRAN) MASHHAD-BELUCHISTAN	BELUCHISTAN
BELUCHISTAN-AFGHAN	

KHIVA BOKHARA. (TOURKOM BOKHARA) Woven by the Kirzig tribe of nomads who live in the province of Northern Turkoman, they are somewhat closely tied and shorter napped than other Turkomans. An octagon design is almost universally employed and is quartered by alternating colours. Lavish use of traditional Turkoman reds in the field, with designs in blue, orange, brown, green and white are features. The largest of the Turkomans, these are one of the best inexpensive rugs.

BESHIR BOKHARA. Woven in five villages on the shores of the Amour River in Turkestan, these are one of the rarest of Turkomans. Designs are usually tree motifs, arranged in strips with alternating coloured ·backgrounds. Caucasian and Mongol symbols are commonly employed. Sometimes, Chinese cloud bands fill the field. The free use of yellow is characteristic. Other colours include browns, brownish reds and blues, with occasional whites.

GUZELLE (TEKKE) BOKHARA. Woven by the Tekke Turkoman tribes, who inhabit an area extending to Afghanistan on the south and Khorasan on ·the west, they are famed for their durability. Elongated octagon forms are arranged in rows alternating with rows of diamond forms with straight lines connecting the centres of the octagon, each of which is divided into four equal parts. In the centre of each octagon is frequently found the eight-pointed star. Colours that predominate include a ground of rich, dark mahogany red with designs in blue, green, orange, old rose, wine and pink.

PRINCESS BOKHARA. Although these prayer rugs are woven by the same tribes, there is no comparison between the two. These fine prayer rugs are nearly always the same size and shape, as they are made for the purpose of hanging over tent openings. Braided cords for hanging them are a feature. The field is often quartered by a Greek Cross and at the top is usually found a small niche. The lower end has a fairly wide space outside the borders which is filled with designs and finished with a wide web, while the upper end finishes with the border stripe. It is usually overcast or turned back and hemmed—a feature seldom found in any other rug. The four quarters of the field are invariably filled with forms resembling candlesticks. Any whites in these rugs are worked with cotton, as it does not turn brown with tent smoke—unlike wool.

YAMUD BOKHARA. Sometimes called the Yellow Bokhara, these rugs are woven by a tribe of nomadic Turkomans who live along the shores of the Caspian Sea, in the western part of Turkestan. Designs show great individuality, with many of them influenced by Caucasian forms. Octagons and elongated diamond patterns in alternate rows with plenty of latch-hook variations are just some of them. Often, the field is covered with diamond forms alone. Ground colours are invariably rich, brownish red, which is softer and deeper than any other Turkoman, while figures tend to be in drab; blue, green and yellow.

KIRGHIS. Woven by the Kirghis tribe from the Steppes to the north of Turkestan, these rugs use highly conventionalized floral forms and Persian garden patterns. Colours are usually red, blue and yellow, with Chinese red dominant. They are frequently referred to as Kazak.

ERSARI. The tribes of Ersari, who live along the Oxas River, weave these rugs. The designs are usually a repetition of stiff little archaic figures. Sometimes octagons carrying small dogs, arrow heads, stars and leaves are employed. Colours are usually Bokhara and Samarkand yellows. A feature of these rugs are that they are completely woven from wool.

SAMARKAND. Named after a city of western Turkestan from whence they come, they usually have a five-medallion motif – one at each corner of the field and one in the centre, which bear dragon, animal or floral forms. There is minimal Persian, Turkish, or Caucasian influence, rather, Mongolian characteristics prevail. Chinese frets, swastikas, dragons, fish and floral forms often fill the borders. The undulating vine and lotus patterns are frequently used. The field is usually blue, red, or golden brown. Bokhara reds and yellows are used with abandon.

KASHGAR. So called after the city of Kashgar in eastern Turkestan – one of the richest markets in Central Asia, the designs of these rugs also bear witness to Chinese influence. Generally, fretted grounds or trellis forms covered with bat, butterfly, crane, dragon, fish and tree forms predominate. The knot of destiny is also used. Strong yellows, blues, reds, with pinks, greens, orange and pale terra cotta are the main colours.

YARKAND. Another eastern Turkestan city, name of Yarkand, is the weaving place for these rugs, which also display Mongol occupation. Designs are similar to those of Bokhara and Kashgar. Fretted grounds with figures of animals, bats, dragons, butterflies, circles and octagons, are to the fore. A common pattern is an arrangement of four dragons to form a swastika. Colours include rich, reddish browns, or occasionally tans, in the field, with blue, red, green, yellow, pink, or terra cotta patternings.

BELUCHISTAN. A vast, wild and mountainous country, extending from Zahedan to Pakistan, and from Afghanistan to the South Arabian Sea, Beluchistan has nevertheless strong traditions as a rug weaving region. Designs are usually geometrical devices – hexagons, octagons, etc., and occasionally stiff floral patterns. Colours are usually dark reds and dark browns with a sprinkling of white. Tan is frequently employed in the field and is generally undyed camels' hair. These rugs are one of the last to be affected by outside influences, tribal patterns, weaving and dyeing being rigidly adhered to. Beluchistan Rugs woven by the tribes in Afghanistan are of a wool base whereas the finer quality rugs woven around Mashhad, in north-eastern Iran, are woven on a cotton base.

NEMAZELIK (PRAYER RUGS)

"And some sigh for the Prophet's Paradise to come;...."

The Rubaiyat of OMAR KHAYYAM

Some thirty classifications of various Nemazelik or Sajadeh patterns are on record, but it would not be an exaggeration to suggest that the actual number of patterns runs into thousands. This is because each time a design is copied, the weaver usually adds his own personality, through his interpretation of that design.

The normal size for a Prayer Rug varies between two feet and six feet square, although larger sizes have been produced—usually more decorative than the smaller variety.

What doesn't often vary is the one-way pattern. This is because the Mehrab, or Head of the rug, where the worshipper places his forehead, hands on either side, always faces East, to Mecca. The basic design used symbolises the main pillars and entrance of a mosque with its chandeliers, which usually hang from the centre of the Mehrab.

Special Mecca Prayer Rugs, known as 'Tribute Rugs', are also woven. As a rule, the Hajis leave these behind at Mecca, after their Haj is completed.

The finest and most beautiful of all prayer rugs, which is always treated with the utmost respect in Iran, is shown on Page one. It is the Shah Abbas Silk Prayer Rug.

HANGING RUGS (BERDELIKE)

"The arras, rich with horseman, hawk and hound,
Fluttered in the besieging wind's uproar;
And the long carpets rose along the dusty floor." . . .

John Keats

Hanging rugs fall mostly within the classification of fine silk rugs. This is because a silk rug when properly hung on the wall with efficent lighting, continuously changes its colours and hues—depending on where the viewer stands — and the sheen has a bewitching quality, especially at night. The themes for hanging rugs vary although Hunting scenes do tend to predominate.

RUNNERS (KENNARE)

Runners, a popular type of woven rug, take many forms and vary in length from 2 feet to 20 feet. They are perfect for corridors and other areas about the house, where there is a lot of traffic, or where a splash of colour is required. Needless to say, they are extremely hard-wearing.

SADDLE BAGS (SEMERLIK)

Saddle bags once provided a dual purpose—firstly as a saddle over cushioned blankets for riding and secondly, as a bag for transporting various wares. In the modern form saddle bags have been converted, so as to be used as Pouffes.

GRAVE OR FUNERAL RUGS

" — And many Knots unravel'd by the Road;
But not the Knots of Human Death and Fate . . ."

The Rubaiyat of OMAR KHAYYAM

By ancient custom, grave rugs are woven only by the dead person's family and relatives. The rug is almost always predominately black, with woven inscriptions from the Koran. Grave Rugs are used to wrap the dead person before burial and are interred with him.

KES KHELIME (WEDDING RUGS)

"A Flask of Wine, a Book of Verse —
and Thou Beside me singing in the Wilderness —
Oh,Wilderness were Paradise enow ! . . . ."

The Rubaiyat of OMAR KHAYYAM

Wedding rugs usually form a wedding dowry from the parents of the bride. The majority of these rugs are jointly commissioned by both the bridegroom's and bride's parents at the couple's betrothal, with an agreement that it be completed by the time the wedding takes place. As betrothals tend to take place at a rather tender age, not only in Iran but throughout the whole of Central Asia, most of these carpets are of great value because of the time it takes to complete them. Some are priceless.

"...And in this fabric is awoven
all man's dreams and aspirations..."

Dryden

SUPREME PERSIAN CARPETS—
A MATTER OF DESIGN

There is little question that design sets the Supreme Persian Carpet apart from all others. And no wonder, because design, especially carpet design, is an art form in which the Persians excel. Their particular gifts include an instinct to formalise any subject — to establish it as a formed pattern according to accepted conventions. They do not regard these conventions as being restrictive in any way, rather, they see them as charming reminders that have survived from bygone generations, which they gladly observe and pass on through their weaving.

Much has been made of symbolism in Persian Carpet design, but I am increasingly of the opinion that it is overplayed. The Persians, with their artistic development, regard design as an end in itself. This is not to say there has been no passing on of design from generation to generation, rather, that seeking to invest meaning into various designs and to attempt to explain them as tribal manifestos would seem pointless, as those meanings are lost in antiquity.

Persian Carpet patterns fall into two broad categories — curvilinear (curved lines) and rectilinear (straight lines). These are largely determined by the two basic techniques of Persian Carpet weaving—the tribal, or village weaves which usually reflect the straight lines and the town, or factory weaves which generally use the curved line, although straight lines are used to delineate borders in both weaves.

Down through the centuries, a number of designs have persisted, nine of which are the most common.

THE HERATI

Perhaps the most widespread, is the Herati. It is also known as the Mahi or Fish pattern. Its beginnings lie in East Persia and more often than not, it takes the form of a well-defined diamond shape, around which, four "fish" are arranged. The Herati pattern is usually combined with the Tosbagheh or "turtle" border. In Tabriz, the border is referred to as the "samovar", which it also closely resembles.

THE BOTEH

This is the fabled Pine Pattern. After the Herati, it is the most wide-spread of all the well-known designs. The word Boteh means "cluster of leaves" and in its simplest form, the design does closely resembled a serrated leaf.

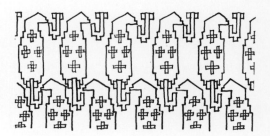

THE HARSHANG

This design takes its name from the principal motif, which resembles a crab—a repetitive pattern that is simple yet full of character. Its origins are lost, however, there are strong Turkish overtones to it, which may suggest its ancestry.

THE GOL HENAI

This small repeating pattern is supposedly named after the Henna plant, which may, or may not, be so. Although it is a well-known pattern in Iran, its use seems to be regional—that of the Mushkabad and Mahal weavers. In the West it is referred to as the "chestnut" pattern because of its resemblance to the horse-chestnut blossom.

THE LECHEK TORUNJ

This is the medallion-and-corner design that is typically Persian, both in elegance and refinement. Its popularity among the weavers of Tabriz, Mashhad and Keriz is because, by following three simple rules, a carpet of pleasing proportions will always result. There are, of course, many variations of the Lechek Torunj.

THE MINA KHANI

This design is supposedly named after a Tabrizi master weaver, who originated and popularized it. It is basically the "Classic Floral" design with a small repeat. Earliest examples of it suggest a Kurdish influence.

THE SHAH ABBAS

The term Shah Abbas defines an all-over design composed of "Classical" motifs of the middle Sefavi period (about 1600). These motifs, which included the various forms of palmettes, cloud bands, halberds and vases were delineated during the reign of Shah Abbas (1587 — 1629). The designs appear in the field of the carpet, isolated from each other, evenly spaced and almost always interlinked into a pattern—by the use of stalk and/or trellis forms. The Shah Abbas are woven all over Iran but nowhere are they seen to more advantage than in Esfahan, the ancient capital of Shah Abbas.

THE BIN MAJNUNZ

The "weeping willow" design is one of the oldest and most famous of the old Persian patterns. It is a combination of the weeping willow, cypress, poplar and fruit trees. Its origins are obscure but again, Kurdish elements are suggested.

THE JOSHAGANI

Named after a village where, for two centuries, two classic lozenge designs have been woven, this pattern sometimes repeats the corner lozenges over the field. There are examples where the medallions have been omitted, sometimes the corners—and often both. Within the lozenges can be found the other classic designs, such as the weeping willow and the Shah Abbas palmettes, etc.

SUPREME PERSIAN CARPETS —
A QUESTION OF COLOUR

The master-dyers of Persia are regarded with a great deal of respect, for theirs is an ancient and revered profession. Indeed, Persian dye-stuffs and dyers are an integral part of the art of Persian Carpet making — as much as the weaving, the materials and the designs.

In the following section, I will discuss the materials used for colouring a Supreme Persian Carpet.

MADDER

The madder plant, which grows wild in most parts of Iran, has been used as a colourant as far back as written history. It is a perennial with a yellow-green flower and a thick pulpy root which sometimes reaches a depth of six feet. The root takes three years to mature underground before it is of any use. It is then dug up, dried, beaten and ground to a coarse powder. The madder plant provides the complete red spectrum, from the deepest reds to the most subtle of pinks.

WELD

This is a thin, delicate plant which also grows wild in most parts of Iran. Its stalks, leaves and flowers provide a yellow dye which is used, both alone and in combinations, to produce other colours.

VINE LEAVES

These are also used for producing yellow dyes — a brighter, less delicate shading that that of the weld plant.

POMEGRANATE RIND

It is abundant and is also used for producing yellows—however, they are usually of a muddy hue and less attractive than those produced from the weld plant and the vine leaves.

WALNUT HUSKS

These are unrivalled for producing beautiful shades of brown. A great variety of hues are produced in combination with madder, weld and other dyestuffs.

OAK BARK

Another regional variant which produces brown shadings.

INDIGO

While not strictly Persian, the indigo plant has been associated with Persian Carpets for centuries. It is cultivated in Khuzistan and produces the most breathtaking of blues.

COCHINEAL

This imported dyestuff which is extracted from shellac — the resinous secretion of a scale insect — is used to produce reds of all types.

NATURAL COLOURS

The whites creams and silvers found in Supreme Persian Carpets are almost always totally natural, in the former two, from the fine belly wool of young lambs and in the latter, from both natural silk and silver thread.

ANILINE DYES

There is always a problem with cheap imported dyes being used by unscrupulous makers. And perhaps only the expert can tell the difference. It is therefore important that you go to a reputable and well-known dealer and ask him to show you examples of the real thing and the aniline-dyed product so that you can learn to note the differences by eye.

SUPREME PERSIAN CARPETS—
THE FABRICS AND THE FIBRES

There are only three of any importance; wool, silk and cotton. Some of the Baluchi tribe utilize goat's hair in their carpet selvedges, while camel's hair, because of a distinctive smell, is hardly ever encountered. Hemp, which is commonly used in India and Pakistan for the weft, is **never** used in Persian Carpet manufacture.

"Belly up, the lamb shall give her wool..."

Arab proverb

WOOL

The quality of wool varies, but universally, the longer the staple, or fibre, the more superior the wool is. The softest and most luxuriant wool is produced by carding sheep in winter. The wool produced in this fashion is known as Kurk and from it, some of the choicest carpet pieces are made.

It is of the greatest importance that the pile be made from the finest quality wool, as it is this portion of the carpet which must bear the heaviest wear-and-tear and abuse. Only wool has the resilience to take the kind of punishment that is usually meted out to a carpet and still spring back, ready to last, from age to age, colours undaunted.

*"Does the silk-worm expend her labours
just for thee? . . . For thee does she undo herself?"*

Rudaki

SILK—A HISTORY

Silk, the wondrous material that gives the finest Supreme Persian Carpets their indescribable sheen and lustre, is perhaps the most incredible material the world has ever known.

The silkworm which produces it, is quite the opposite, being as it is, a rather nondescript little creature, ashy-white to yellow in colour, which spends most of its life gorging itself on the leaves of the mulberry tree. When the worm is mature, it spins a cocoon, which in fact is an unbroken thread of silk, varying between 800 and 1200 yards in length.

To the best of our knowledge, the art of silk gathering and weaving had its beginnings in Ancient China. There, more than 4000 years ago, a Chinese Empress discovered the secrets of the silk-worm. She experimented until she found the method of recovering this fine fibre — by killing the silk-worm moth while it was still inside the cocoon. After her death, Chinese silk workers installed her as their patron saint, naming her 'The Goddess of Silk'. Her name continued to be venerated until, in 1742, the Emperor of the time, Chien Lung ordered a shrine be constructed in her honour in Peking—a fitting tribute to one who gave silk to the world.

For many years, the art of silk making was a jealously guarded secret, and woe betide anyone who gave it away. By Imperial Decree, he or she would be horribly tortured and then put to death.

In spite of these precautions, the secret of silk was soon transported to other lands. About 775, two Persian monks, who had learned the art in China, arrived in Constantinople, complete with a precious cargo of silk-worm eggs hidden in bamboo canes. It is from these eggs incidentally, that all the races and varieties of silk-worms evolved, which were to supply the Western World with silk for the next 1200 years.

Over the centuries, silk-weaving flourished in Persia, Palestine, Egypt and Syria. So much so, that Byzantine silks became world-renowned and in great demand.

The artists involved in the creation of Persian Carpets soon realised the value of using this unique fibre in their carpets and today, these carpets serve as testament, to the supreme artistry of the carpet makers and that nondescript little insect, the silk-worm.

"Cotton, white upon the boll ′ . . ."

Firdausi

COTTON

Cotton is produced in many areas of Iran; in fact, there is hardly a province that does not grow it. However, principal production of cotton takes place in Esfahan, Kashan, Kazvin, Yezd, Mashhad and Kirman provinces.

Cotton has been proven to be the most suitable material for the warps and wefts of hand-knotted carpets because, unlike wool, it does not shrink unevenly and it provides a surface tension that grips any flooring.

Handspun cotton is used almost exclusively for the cheaper grades of rugs and carpets, mainly because it is a product of village industry. Millspun cotton is normally used in the urban and semi-urban carpets. This is again because of availability.

THE WEAVING OF A SUPREME PERSIAN CARPET

THE LOOMS
Four different types of loom are used in Iran:

THE GROUND LOOM
Light and portable, the ground loom is not supported by side pieces. Instead, the two beams are kept apart by stakes driven into the ground. The tension is maintained by driving wedges between the ends of the loom beams and the stakes.

Its advantage for the nomad is that it can be moved at short notice. The unfinished rug is just rolled up on the beams and slung on the back of a transport animal. Its main disadvantage is that a beam over 5ft. in length is impractical to move. For this reason, most tribal rugs are 4 feet or under, in width.

THE UPRIGHT LOOM
1) **The Village Loom** is both the simplest and in many ways the crudest. It consists of a fixed top, or warp beam, and a lower, or cloth beam. The weaver sits on an adjustable plank, which he raises as he moves upwards, until sometimes, he is 5 to 6 feet in the air!

2) **The Tabriz Loom** has many advantages over the Village variety in that the woven part can be slid up behind the loom as it is completed. In this fashion, the weaver works at one height only.

3) **The Roller Beam Loom** is more advanced that the previous two, in that it can take a carpet of almost any length; a greater, more constant tension can be maintained; and it produces straighter-edged carpets than the other types.

THE WEAVERS' TOOLS
A few simple instruments are all the expert weavers need. They consist of: a knife for cutting off the yarn after the knot is made; a beater to beat in the wefts; and a pair of shears for trimming the carpet after it is completed. In Tabriz, instead of using their fingers to pull the knot, the weavers have devised a button hook/knife arrangement which they maintain allows them to knot faster.

THE KNOTS
There are two basic knots employed in the making of Supreme Persian Carpets. They are: the Turki or Turkish knot; (sometimes known, although fallaciously as the Ghiordes knot) and the Farsi or Persian knot. (This is also known, just as wrongly, as the Senneh knot)

THE WEAVING
Weaving, or knotting is done in rows, from side to side. At the end of each row, the weaver beats each weft up tight to the preceding weft and then trims the pile. The pattern is built up by the use of dyed wools. When finished, the rug or carpet is knotted to an embroidery piece to make the finished article a little more beautiful. A selvedge is also formed at the carpet's side by knotting.

SUPREME PERSIAN CARPETS— HOW TO CARE FOR THEM

TO BRUSH OR VACUUM?

The method of cleaning your Supreme Persian Carpet is largely a matter of choice. It certainly does no harm to either brush the carpet with a stiff broom, or to vacuum-clean it. One good idea is to vacuum the underside of the carpet once a year, as dirt and grit tend to lodge in the base. One should also try to brush or vacuum, with the weft and then, against it.

WASHING

As a general rule, you should sponge your carpet at least once a year, using plain soap and water. Do not be overly concerned if the colours of your carpet run. This is quite normal and in fact it helps a young carpet by washing off excessive dyestuffs.

DAMPNESS, EXCESSIVE HUMIDITY, ETC.

The cure is simple, if any of these conditions are present, just place the carpet in the sun, bottom side up, for two or three hours a week. Newspaper, placed under the carpet, is extremely useful, as it absorbs moisture and prevents it from penetrating the fabric.

MOTH & INSECT PROOFING

Any of the reputable moth and insect-proofing formulae can be used without any qualms. And they should be applied at least once a year. Over-soaking is not a problem, but you should treat the underside of the carpet, before the pile.

SPOT CLEANING

Certain types of spots can be removed without cleaning the complete rug. If it is a grease spot, commercial spot cleaners will achieve the desired result. But take care! Most foods cause little problem, in that they do not penetrate. A wipe with a damp cloth is usually sufficient.

Coffee and soft drinks do present problems, as the former tends to set, while the latter causes faded spots. The treatment for both is sponging with plain cold water — as soon as possible. It is also advisable to go over the section with soap and water afterwards.

An ink spot can be taken out by first pouring milk on it, then scooping both the milk and ink up with a spoon. This will remove most of the stain. Then wash with soap and water.

BLEACHING

Chemical Bleaching is not advisable as this can completely ruin your carpet. There is no more efficient bleaching agent than the sun — and plenty of it.

PROFESSIONAL CLEANERS

It is not advisable to send your carpet to a professional cleaner, without checking them out very thoroughly. The reason is, that most rug cleaners force dry carpets, which can have bad effects on the colouration of your carpet — especially cotton fringes. In most cases, if you don't mind the labour of love, you can do a better job at home. So, only really dirty carpets should be sent out, but do insist that they be thoroughly rinsed after washing and that they be dried in the sun.

LEAVE IT TO THE EXPERTS.

If your Supreme Persian Carpet is in a really bad condition and the available professional carpet cleaners do not inspire you with confidence—don't despair. There are four expert companies in the world which can help restore your rug to its former glory—although the process is necessarily expensive.

In England, it is Abadijians in Harrow, which company was established some 40 years ago.

In Switzerland, it is Terlinden & Co., Zurich.

In Germany and Austria, it is Migo of Hamburg, Dusseldorf and Vienna.

In Australia, New Zealand and Asia, it is **Oriental Carpet Palace** of Singapore, through its partners and agents in Tehran.

Each of these companies has both the necessary equipment of the specialised type, and the expertise to help. A step-by-step procedure is invariably followed. **First:** the rugs are beaten in special beating machines which are fully enclosed, but which have observation chambers for the operators. Vacuum-operated extractors remove all the dust released by the beating operation. **Second:** the rug is examined by an expert, to ascertain the next treatment necessary to achieve the desired results. **Third:** the carpet is washed, sometimes in water, other times in chemicals. After treatment, all the water and chemical residues are completely removed—usually through centrifugal force. **Fourth:** Now comes the tricky part—drying. The carpets are passed slowly through a special drying chamber, in a horizontal position. During this process, both temperature and humidity are strictly controlled.

Fifth: the rugs are put through a shearing machine which lightly shears them — to correct any unevenness in the pile.

Sixth: the carpets are checked again, usually for binding faults and uneven fringes, but also for possible discolouration or washing out— both of which can be rectified.

Seventh: this last special process imparts a beautiful and long-lasting lustre to the wool pile and then the carpets are ready to be returned to their owners—like new again!

SUPREME PERSIAN CARPETS —
THE FUTURE

There is no question that the purchase of a
Supreme Persian Carpet is a major expenditure and as the
carpets appreciate, it becomes even more so.

It is therefore most important that you make your
purchase from a reputable Persian Carpet Dealer and
that the Persian Carpet be woven in Iran,
and not elsewhere.

THE BUYER'S CHECKLIST

1. Is the rug very irregular in shape?

Slight irregularities are to be expected in hand-woven rugs, but excessive irregularities should not be entertained. Carpets can be professionally stretched to improve in their shape, however.

2. Does the rug lie flat?

Don't let anyone tell you that wrinkles will walk out; unless professionally stretched, they won't!

3. Is the rug unevenly clipped?

If so, the re-sale value will reduced, unless the carpet is professionally sheared or shaved.

4. Are the colours running excessively?

Bad stains also reduce re-sale values.

5. Is the rug a genuine hand-woven rug?

Check the underside of the carpet. All hand-made carpets show their pattern and colouring clearly on the reverse side, whereas machine-made ones do not.

6. Is the price right?

Don't buy without checking out similar rugs at two or more dealers. Reputable dealers will not object to you doing a price comparison.

7. Will it fit?

Fitting or fitting in, make sure the carpet of your choice will physically fit where you want it to, and be sure that it also works in with the surroundings. Most dealers will allow you to have a rug at home on approval, and will refund your money if you find the carpet isn't suitable.

TREE OF LIFE

WE, THE UNDERSIGNED, DECLARE WITH TRUTH AND FAITH THAT NURE MOHD. KHAN S/o GUL MOHD. KHAN IS AN AFGHAN AND RESIDENT OF KABUL. HIS ANCESTORS ABDICATED ALONG WITH HAZRAT SHAH SHAJAH, THE KING OF AFGHANISTAN, AND THEY HAVE TAKEN THEIR RESIDENCE IN LUDHIANA. HIS PEDIGREE IS AS FOLLOWS:—

GHULAM REZA KHAN

SULTAN MOHD. KHAN   GUL MOHD. KHAN   TAJ MOHD. KHAN

AMIR MOHD. KHAN   NURE MOHD. KHAN

SO WE HAVE WRITTEN THESE LINES AS A TESTIMONY.

DATED 4TH MARCH 1899.

SIGNED BY:—

SH. SAEED AHMAD	MIRZA MOHD. ISMAIL	MOHD. HASHIM KHAN
AMIR-UL-LAH KHAN	MOHD. SHAH	MIRZA HASSAN ALI
MIRZA MOHD. SAEED	ABDUL RAHIM	SHEHZADA AZIZUDIN
	MOHD. KHAN	

هم گواه سندات .... ست بیان کرتے ہیں اپنے اف ایمان اگر انگرکی

نصدیق کرتے ہیں کہ نور محمد خان ولد گل محمد خان قوم افغان اور کابل کا شند

اوسکی بزرگان کابل سے حضرت شاہ شجاع الملک بادشاہ خان ستان کے ساتھ جلا وطن

ہوکر آئی بن اور ان کی ساتھ دلو دیا نہ زمین طرب سے سکونت کبھی بن اور کا تجدد ت

عبدل سرت   شمگلو .... علے

مورشد علے

قائم رضا خان

حاج محمد خان   گل محمد خان   سلطان محمد خان

نور محمد خان   امیر محمد خا

لکھنو عہد کمال طرتی محبر ناصر خان یا صورت خان کے لکد ملکہ سند واد عبد الی

کام اودی المرقوم ۱۴ ماچ سن ۹۹ ء

عبد ک   نسبت ....   عبد ک   گرص نظم خو

The publisher of this book was awarded
a specially minted gold medal by Her Imperial Majesty,
the Shahbanou of Iran, for his contribution towards
the promotion of Iranian culture and handicraft.

1747. A year of great significance in Afghanistan. Ahmad Khan Abdali was elected King of the Afghans by a tribal assembly and established the Durrani Dynasty. A capable ruler he welded his people into a strong nation and liberated Afghanistan from foreign rule. His achievements won him the title of 'Father of the Nation'.

On his death, his son Timur succeeded him. Following the death of Timur in 1793, his fifth son, Zaman, seized the throne. After a series of royal intrigues, Zaman was betrayed and his elder brother, Mahmud became king.

Mahmud was an indolent ruler who squandered the nation's treasures and created unrest throughout the country. Finally, some of the chiefs joined forces and, led by Shah Shuja, a full brother of Zaman, invaded the capital. Mahmud sued for peace. His life was spared but he was imprisoned in Kabul.

The new king, Shah Shuja, who ascended to the throne in 1803, ruled for eight years before he was overthrown by Mahmud. Shah Shuja found asylum under the British at Ludhiana in the Indian state of Punjab along with his family, including a brother **Ghulam Reza Khan.** Shortly after, the Durrani Dynasty was ended.

Ghulam Reza Khan's son, Gul Mohamed Khan eventually returned to Afghanistan and became a resident of Kabul and it was here that his son, **Haji Amir Mohamed Khan** was born.

Little wonder then, that **Haji Amir Mohamed Khan,** whose ancestry was steeped in the glories of Afghanistan and Persia, which were closely linked historically, should have fallen in love with Supreme Persian Carpets. He became one of the leading merchants in this field.

The traditions and secrets of this ancient craft are jealously upheld and guarded in turn by his son today, **Haji Mohamed Khan Zephyr Amir** — recognised as the most knowledgeable authority on Supreme Persian Carpets in South-east Asia, Australasia and the Pacific region.

INDEX